A Note fi
Mary Pope Osborn

When I write Magic Tree House® adventures, I love including facts about the times and places Jack and Annie visit. But when readers finish these adventures, I want them to learn even more. So that's why we write a series of nonfiction books that are companions to the fiction titles in the Magic Tree House® series. We call these books Fact Trackers because we love to track the facts! Whether we're researching dinosaurs, pyramids, Pilgrims, sea monsters, or cobras, we're always amazed at how wondrous and surprising the real world is. We want you to experience the same wonder we do—so get out your pencils and notebooks and hit the trail with us. You can be a Magic Tree House® Fact Tracker, too!

Mary Pope Osborne

Here's what kids, parents, and teachers have to say about the Magic Tree House® Fact Trackers:

"They are so good. I can't wait for the next one. All I can say for now is prepare to be amazed!" —Alexander N.

"I have read every Magic Tree House book there is. The [Fact Trackers] are a thrilling way to get more information about the special events in the story." —John R.

"These are fascinating nonfiction books that enhance the magical time-traveling adventures of Jack and Annie. I love these books, especially *American Revolution.* I was learning so much, and I didn't even know it!" —Tori Beth S.

"[They] are an excellent 'behind-the-scenes' look at what the [Magic Tree House fiction] has started in your imagination! You can't buy one without the other; they are such a complement to one another." —Erika N., mom

"Magic Tree House [Fact Trackers] took my children on a journey from Frog Creek, Pennsylvania, to so many significant historical events! The detailed manuals are a remarkable addition to the classic fiction Magic Tree House books we adore!" —Jenny S., mom

"[They] are very useful tools in my classroom, as they allow for students to be part of the planning process. Together, we find facts in the [Fact Trackers] to extend the learning introduced in the fictional companions. Researching and planning classroom activities, such as our class Olympics based on facts found in *Ancient Greece and the Olympics,* help create a genuine love for learning!" —Paula H., teacher

Horse Heroes

A NONFICTION COMPANION TO
MAGIC TREE HOUSE MERLIN MISSION #21:
Stallion by Starlight

BY MARY POPE OSBORNE
AND NATALIE POPE BOYCE

ILLUSTRATED BY SAL MURDOCCA

A STEPPING STONE BOOK™
Random House New York

The Magic Tree House Fact Tracker series was formerly known as the Magic Tree House Research Guide series. Magic Tree House Merlin Mission #21 was formerly known as Magic Tree House #49.

Visit us on the Web!
SteppingStonesBooks.com
randomhousekids.com
MagicTreeHouse.com

Educators and librarians, for a variety of teaching tools, visit us at
RHTeachersLibrarians.com

Library of Congress Cataloging-in-Publication Data
Osborne, Mary Pope.
Horse heroes / by Mary Pope Osborne and Natalie Pope Boyce ;
illustrated by Sal Murdocca.
p. cm. — (Magic tree house fact tracker)
Includes index.
"A nonfiction companion to Magic tree house, #49: Stallion by Starlight."
ISBN 978-0-375-87026-2 (trade) — ISBN 978-0-375-97026-9 (lib. bdg.) —
ISBN 978-0-375-98863-9 (ebook)
1. Horses—Juvenile literature. 2. Animal heroes—Juvenile literature.
I. Boyce, Natalie Pope. II. Murdocca, Sal, ill. III. Title.
SF302.O73 2013 636.1—dc23 2012021961

Printed in the United States of America
15 14 13 12 11 10 9

This book has been officially leveled by using the F&P Text Level Gradient™ Leveling System.

For Jean Sorenson, with gratitude and love for her years in the classroom

Scientific and Historical Consultant:
JESSIE HAAS, author of *Horse Crazy! 1,001 Fun Facts, Craft Projects, Games, Activities, and Know-How for Horse-Loving Kids*

Education Consultant:
HEIDI JOHNSON, language acquisition and science education specialist, Bisbee, Arizona

Special thanks to Vicky Cooper and Diablo, and that great Random House gang: Gloria Cheng; Mallory Loehr; Chelsea Eberly; Sal Murdocca for the brilliant art; and our wonderful editor, Diane Landolf, who probably needs a long rest after this book

HORSE HEROES

Contents

Dear Readers,

In Stallion by Starlight, we met Alexander the Great and his horse, Bucephalus. Bucephalus was Alexander's faithful friend. In fact, nobody but Alexander could ride him. Alexander rode into many battles with Bucephalus and even built a temple named to honor him when he died.

Some people say that after horses were tamed, the world changed forever. We were curious to know if this was true. It was time to track the facts!

It surprised us to find out that horses are one of the most important animals in human history. We read that at first people hunted

horses for food. Later, horses helped people get around. They worked on farms and delivered mail. They carried soldiers into battle and explorers into strange lands. They have also played a big role in sports.

Bucephalus was a great horse, but other horses were really wonderful, too. So get out your notebooks, head to your library and to your computer, and let's gallop with the horses!

Jack
Annie

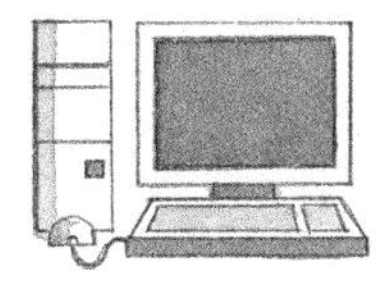

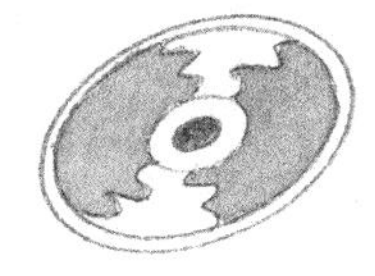

1

Horses

Horses and people have been together for thousands of years. Before we tamed horses, we walked almost everywhere we went. There were no cars or airplanes to help us get around. Having horses to carry us and pull our carts changed the way we lived.

Horses made it easier for us to explore and settle new lands. They helped us share news over long distances. Horses worked on farms and took our goods to market. Soldiers charged into battle with horses as their loyal companions. Horses have also long been an important part of sporting events, especially horse racing.

Over the years, we've told stories, created art, and sung songs about the way horses have touched our lives. No animals have ever worked harder for us than horses. Even though there aren't as many jobs for them now, the bond between humans and horses is as strong as ever.

Wild at Heart

For millions of years, horses were wild and lived in herds. They were prey animals that stayed alert for enemies. Horses survived by running away from danger.

Instinct is a natural behavior that animals are born with.

Today horses are still born to run. Their *instinct* to escape is as strong as it was millions of years ago.

Great Legs

A running horse is a picture of grace and speed. A horse can go from standing to a full gallop in just seconds. Its legs are designed to run fast. Compared to its heavy body, a horse's legs are thin.

Strong muscles, tendons, and joints in the legs all work together to help horses reach top speeds in a short time. The only muscle in their legs is a large one above the knees. Tendons in the lower legs connect to the bones. They help horses move smoothly.

A horse's body parts are called its points.

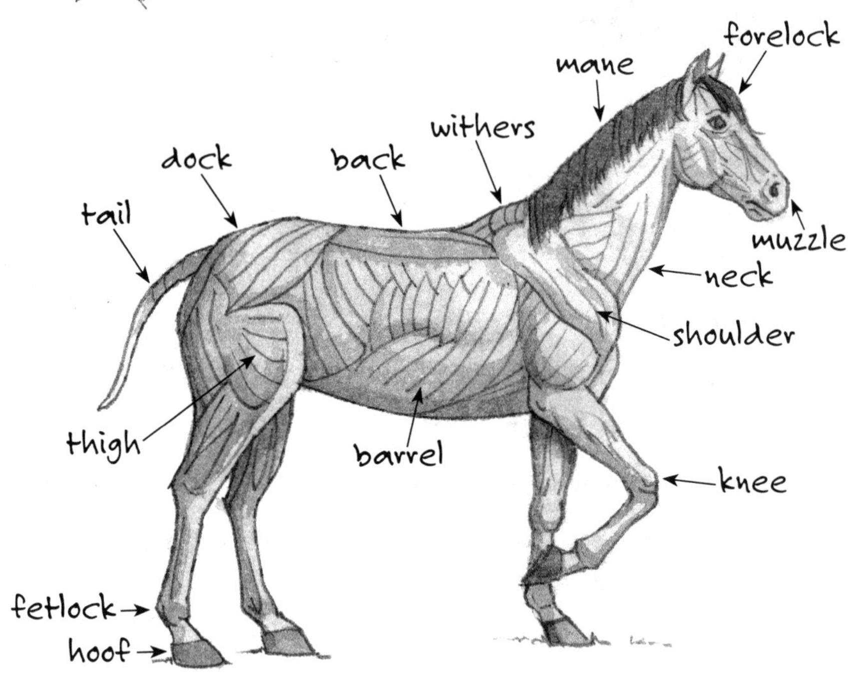

A stride is one complete forward movement.

Because their legs are long, horses can cover a lot of ground in just one *stride*. When they gallop, a single stride can clear twenty-two feet!

Hooves

A popular saying among horse lovers is "No hoof, no horse!" Without healthy hooves, horses can't walk or run well. In fact, they might not be able to walk at all.

A horse's hoof is actually a single toe. It walks on tiptoes, like a ballet dancer. If we ran like a horse, all our weight would be on our middle fingers and middle toes!

Hooves are like our fingernails and hair. They never stop growing. Moving around wears down the hooves and keeps them from getting too long.

Horses that often walk over hard surfaces need metal horseshoes to protect their hooves. Horseshoes also help them move better and improve the way they stand.

Don't worry, it doesn't hurt! There are no nerves where the nails are.

A horseshoe is shaped like a U and usually made of steel. Nails hammered into the horseshoes around the edges of the hooves keep the shoes from falling off.

Horses' hooves should be cleaned out often. Stones and mud can get in them and cause problems. Careful owners check their horses' hooves each day and have new horseshoes put on about every six weeks.

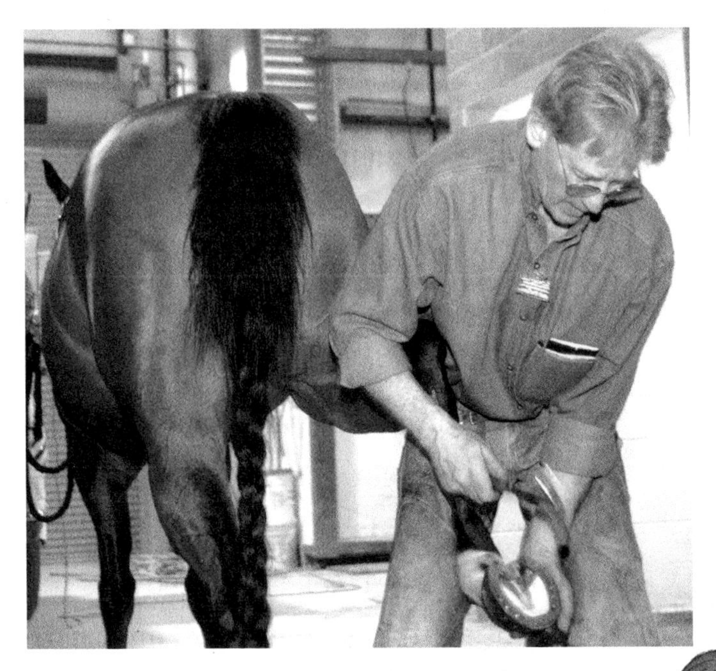

Farriers put shoes on horses and take care of their hooves.

Gaits

Horses have different ways of moving forward. Each of these movements is called a *gait*. Most horses use only three—walk, trot, and canter.

The slowest gait is a walk. When a horse

walks, it puts one foot down at a time. A healthy horse walks about four miles an hour.

The second gait is called a trot. A trot is about eight miles an hour. That's about twice as fast as a human can walk. Most horses can trot for hours at a time.

A canter is faster than a trot. Depending on its stride, a horse covers ten to seventeen miles an hour when it canters. A gallop is a fast canter. A healthy horse gallops about thirty miles an hour! Horses can't run this fast for a long time. They need to slow down and rest after a mile or two.

The fastest racehorses can reach forty-five miles an hour.

There are lots of other gaits, too, such as the pace, the rack, and the running walk. Some breeds are known for these special gaits.

All four feet lift off the ground at the same time in the course of a gallop.

Breathing

A horse breathes only through its nose, not its mouth. A running horse needs a lot of oxygen, but it can't breathe whenever it wants to. It can only take in air with each stride.

The horse's large nostrils help it take in extra air.

The horse inhales when the back legs move forward and exhales when its front legs touch the ground. At a fast gallop, a horse takes in about fifteen gallons of oxygen a minute!

A horse's teeth take up more room in its head than its brain.

Teeth

Horses need large, strong teeth to chew the tough grasses they eat. Their teeth, like their hooves, never stop growing. Grass has tiny pieces of *silica* in it. Silica is what some sand is made of. When a horse eats grass, the silica grinds down its teeth.

Horses have upper lips designed to take hold of grass. They eat it right down to the ground. While eating, they grind up not only silica but gritty pieces of dirt as well.

Horses usually live twenty-five to thirty years. But one in England named Old Billy died at sixty-two!

Experts can often tell the age of a horse by looking at the wear on its teeth. The teeth get longer and darker as they age.

Eyes

Horses have the largest eyes of all land animals, even bigger than elephants! Their eyes are far apart, on either side of their heads. Because of this, horses don't see the way we do. It's difficult for them to judge distances. Something that moves suddenly like a waving flag or a leaf can cause them to panic.

Horses usually have brown eyes, but they can also be blue, green, amber, or hazel.

A horse can't see what is right behind

it. It might kick when someone walks too close to its back end. Never, ever approach a horse from the rear. You could get kicked!

What's amazing is that a horse can see things around it without turning its head. It can even look in different directions at the same time! A horse lifts up its head to see things in the distance and lowers it to look at things more closely.

Diet

Horses have small stomachs for their size. Since they can only eat little amounts of food at one time, they nibble on grass throughout the day. Their owners often feed them oats, corn, barley, wheat, and hay. The average horse weighs between 900 and 1,100 pounds.

A thousand-pound horse eats about twenty pounds of food a day!

Horses drink a lot of water. In cold

weather, they drink five to ten gallons a day. If they are exercising in the heat, they gulp down about twenty gallons!

Coats

Horses come in different colors. The most common are brown, white, black, gray, and cream.

Besides people, horses are the only other animals that sweat a lot through their skin. Sweating cools them down.

Their coats keep them warm in the winter and cool in the summer. When the weather gets cold, their hair becomes thicker and rougher. They also grow a layer of long, shaggy hair to trap in extra heat.

In the spring, horses shed their winter coats. The new hair grows back sleek and shiny.

Owners sometimes put blankets on their horses in very cold weather.

Words for Horses
Is that a baby horse over there?
No, buckaroo. It's a pony, a type of horse that's sma
even when it's full-grown. Now, here's what we horse folks call other horses!

Word	Meaning
mare	female horse
stallion	male horse
foal	horse under one year old
pony	small horse
filly	young female horse
colt	young male horse

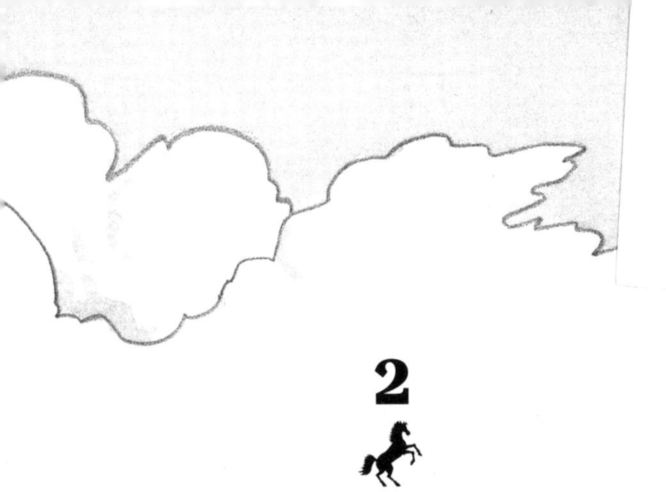

2

Horse Behavior

When horses were wild, the whole herd stayed alert for predators. The watchful eyes of many horses helped each horse's chance of survival.

No matter how tame they are, horses still feel better around other horses. They will groom each other with their teeth and play together.

Horses often give us clues to how they feel. Good riders know their horses and understand their body language.

Tails

A horse's tail is its flyswatter. A horse in a pasture will brush its tail from side to side to keep biting insects away.

Sometimes horses brush flies off each other with their tails.

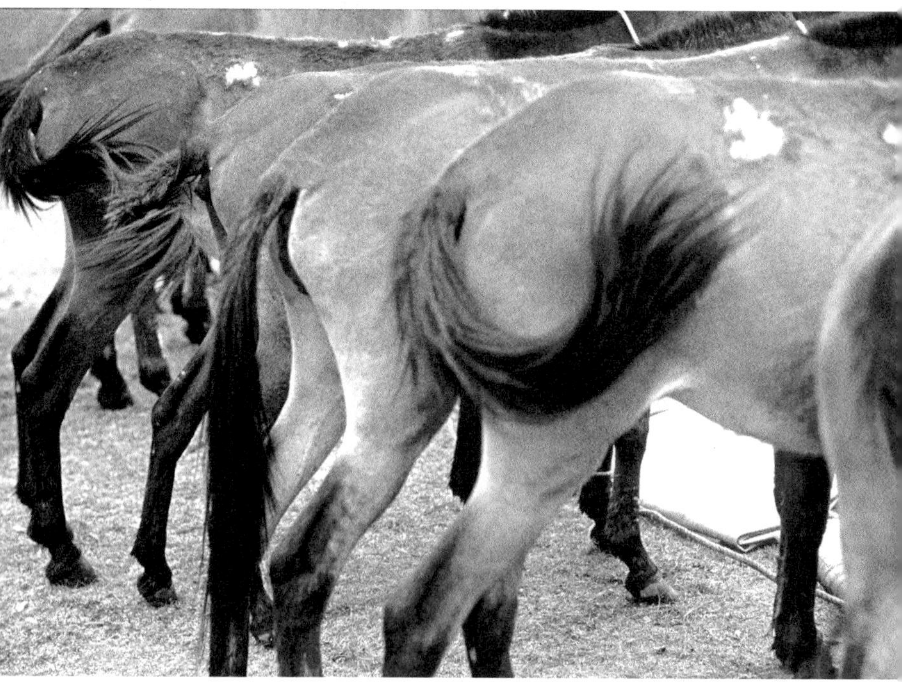

The tail also signals a horse's feelings. If a horse is cold or not well, it might tuck its tail under its body. A calm horse has a droopy, relaxed tail. When a horse is cheerful or excited, its tail is higher than usual. If a horse doesn't want to do what its rider wants, it will swish its tail around a lot. But when a horse whips its tail wildly, better watch out! That horse might buck or kick!

An angry horse often stomps its back feet as well.

Sounds

Horses make several different sounds. There's a soft blowing sound when they greet each other. When strange horses meet, they sometimes squeal as a way of showing that they are ready to defend themselves.

Horses often snort loudly when they're alarmed. They make this sound

A snort can be heard over 200 yards away.

Foals love to play-fight. You guys, stop horsing around!

by exhaling hard through their noses. Then they might turn and stare hard at whatever is bothering them. If they're scared enough, they'll zoom off in the opposite direction!

Horses neigh or whinny when they greet other horses or people. They also whinny to find each other, to get people's attention, or to warn of danger. When horses fight, they let out powerful screams and try to bite each other.

Smell

Horses have a great sense of smell. Their noses tell them if water is fit to drink or if a predator is lurking nearby. They can memorize the smell of other horses and people, too. When horses meet, they touch noses so they can get a good sniff of each other.

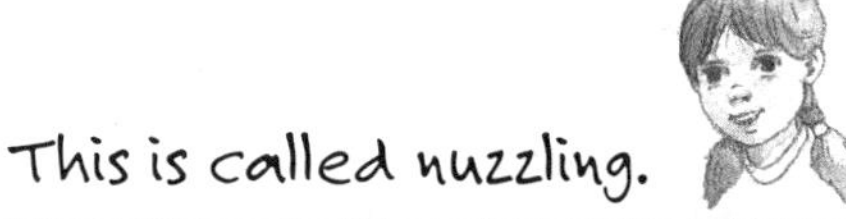
This is called nuzzling.

Since every horse has its own special scent, mares can find their foals among many other horses just by sniffing the air.

People have special smells, too. A horse will often stretch its nose out to smell someone. If you trust the horse, lift your fist up to its nose to let it get to know you.

Ears

Horses hear much better than humans do. Their ears rotate so that they can pick up the smallest sounds. Like their tails, horses' ears tell a lot about their feelings.

They point their ears toward sounds that interest them. When a horse is angry, its ears lie flat and tight against its head. One ear turned to the back means the horse is listening for sounds from behind.

When a horse is paying attention to

its rider, its ears are drawn slightly to the back. Both ears pointing forward usually means that the horse is feeling cheerful and at ease.

Standing Up to Sleep

Horses usually nap standing up so they can escape quickly if they're threatened. Joints in their legs lock into place and keep them from falling over while they doze.

Horses sleep lightly for only about four hours a day. They will sometimes lie down for forty-five minutes or so to get a deeper sleep. When horses are together, one usually remains standing to watch for danger.

Mares and Foals

Most foals are born at night. Right after the baby is born, its mother licks it to encourage it to stand up and nurse. Although a foal is wobbly at first, it trots and gallops the first day! A new foal's legs are almost as long as its mother's.

Mares are very connected to their foals. For the first few weeks, they stay close together, and the mares often lick and nuzzle them.

Buck Brannaman is a famous horse trainer. Buck and his brother grew up around ranches and horses. After their mother died, Buck's father often beat his sons. A sheriff found out about this and sent the boys to a good foster home.

Buck always loved horses. He knew people often trained them by hitting and yelling at them. Because of his childhood, Buck felt strongly that horses could learn faster if they were treated kindly.

When Buck works with horses, he speaks softly. He has learned how horses feel and what scares them. Buck puts the horse at ease as he trains it. He gives classes to show people how to train their horses with understanding and firmness. A movie, *Buck*, was made about him and his training methods.

3

History of Horses

Since 1994, scientists have been studying an ancient site in Kazakhstan (KAH-zack-stan), a country on the border of China and Russia. The site, called Krasnyi Yar, had been a small village where the Botai people lived thousands of years ago.

The Botai hunted wild horses for food. Large herds grazed on the scrubby grasses covering the land and thrived in the cold, thin air.

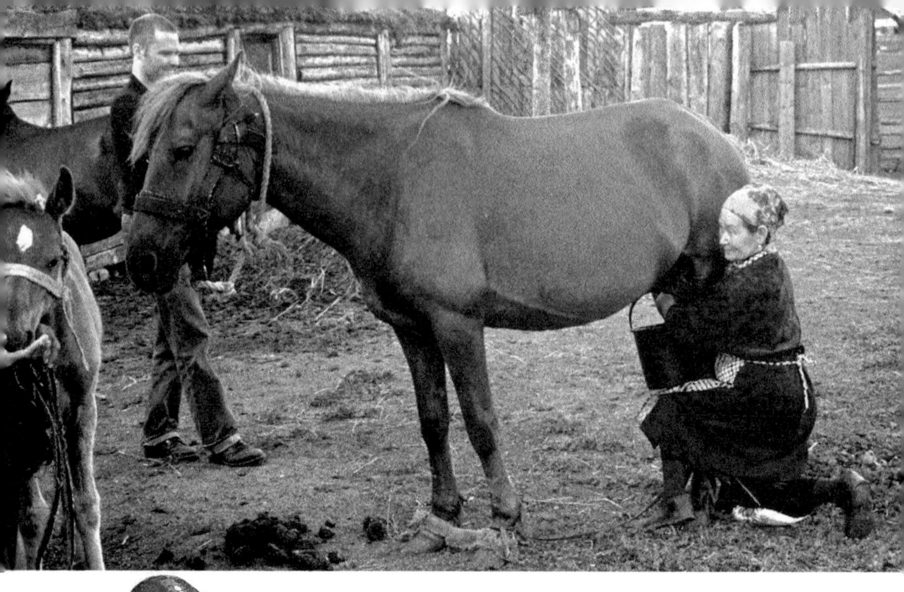

They still milk horses in Kazakhstan today.

As the team carefully sifted through the dirt, they found pieces of pottery and thousands of horse bones and teeth that dated back over 5,500 years. When they tested the pottery, there were traces of fat from mare's milk on it. This was proof that the Botai milked horses and that mare's milk was part of their diet.

Bits fit into a horse's mouth and attach to straps so people can control them.

The horses' teeth showed wear from *bits* that had been in their mouths. The bits meant that the Botai might have used horses for pulling loads or riding.

The Botai find was exciting. No one knew for sure when people began taming horses. The Botai may have been the very first!

Breeding Horses

By 4,000 years ago, people all over Asia and Europe had horses. They started to breed horses to do different things. Some horses became lighter and faster. Others became stronger and larger.

Certain jobs called for fast horses that were easy to ride. These horses carried messengers or were racehorses. Soldiers needed powerful warhorses. They had to be strong enough to pull chariots or carry knights in heavy armor into battle. Farmers needed slow, steady horses, with powerful shoulders to pull plows and farm wagons.

Arabians are among the oldest breeds. Thousands of years ago, tribes in the Middle East wanted light, fast horses to take on raids or into battle. Arabian horses are still popular today. Many of the finest racehorses have Arabian blood.

Arabians are known for their beauty and swiftness.

Horses are measured in <u>hands</u>. A hand is four inches. Fifteen hands high is sixty inches tall from the ground to the top of the withers. (That's five feet tall.)

In the time of knights and castles, knights rode a type of warhorse called a *destrier* (DES-tree-er). Destriers weighed twice as much as other horses. They had extra strength to carry knights wearing heavy armor into battle.

Farmers wanted large horses for farmwork. Many of the biggest horses today come from hundreds of years of careful breeding. The largest, tallest, and strongest workhorse is the *Shire* horse. The English have been breeding Shires for 800 years. They can weigh more than 2,200 pounds and be over twenty hands high!

Among the fastest horses today are Thoroughbreds. Thoroughbreds are relatives of Arabians. The English began breeding them for racing in the 1600s. They are still racing today. These tall, light horses usually reach speeds of about forty miles an hour. There are millions of Thoroughbreds all over the world.

Noddy is a huge Shire, 20.2 hands high, or 6 feet 8 inches tall!

Today there are about three hundred different breeds of horses. Horses changed people, but people changed horses as well!

Mustangs and Native Americans

Spanish explorers first brought horses to the Americas in the 1400s and 1500s. Some escaped and ran wild. By the late 1600s, herds of Spanish horses galloped across the American West. These wild horses are called *mustangs*. Many still exist.

Some Native American tribes began capturing and taming horses. The Comanche, the Shoshone, and the Nez Perce were fantastic bareback riders. The Nez Perce were also great horse breeders.

Native Americans hunted buffalo and went into battle against other tribes on horseback. They could shoot arrows quickly while riding at a gallop.

Some tribes measured their wealth by horses. Horse stealing was common. It became a way for a young warrior to prove he was a man.

Horses were so prized that many tribes had special ceremonies to honor their spirits. Today many Native Americans still own horses, and many are still great riders!

4

Horses Deliver!

Imagine life two or three thousand years ago. People lived in remote villages or on lonely farms. There were no phones, computers, or postal service. Since there were no cars, there weren't even many roads. News from the outside world could take months or years to reach them.

Kings often ruled over vast lands. It took a very long time for them to let their people know about things like new taxes or wars. The use of horses to deliver information helped join people together. It also helped rulers to govern better. They began building roads that connected towns and villages.

Governments sent riders called *couriers* (KER-ee-erz) to deliver official news from one place to another. People also hired couriers to take letters to their friends and relatives. The world began to open up, and we owe much of it to horses.

Persia is another name for Iran.

The Royal Road

Darius, the king of *Persia,* ruled over 2,000 years ago. He built the Royal Road, which ran through much of his kingdom. The road was about 1,677 miles long and went from what is now Turkey to Iraq.

The Persians were among the first

to breed horses for speed and strength. Darius set up a system of couriers to deliver mail on horseback.

King Darius used a seal that showed him in a chariot pulled by a Persian horse—a very small, beautiful breed.

He built over one hundred stations along the Royal Road. Riders stopped at them to pick up mail and fresh horses. It took them about seven days to cover the whole route. It would have taken over ninety days on foot.

The ancient Greek writer Herodotus wrote that nothing—neither snow nor rain nor heat nor dark of night—could stop these brave couriers and their horses. The United States Postal Service uses this as its motto today.

The Cursus Publicus

The ancient Roman Empire covered thousands of miles. Roman rulers needed fast couriers on horseback to carry messages from Rome to distant parts of the empire.

Like King Darius, the Romans began building roads. Over time, their roads covered about 50,000 miles! Remains of these roads still exist today.

The builders put special pavers or stones on the roads to make smoother riding for chariots.

The system set up by the Romans over 1,200 years ago was called the *cursus publicus*, or the public road. They had stations and forts all along the way. Riders with government messages covered about fifty miles a day.

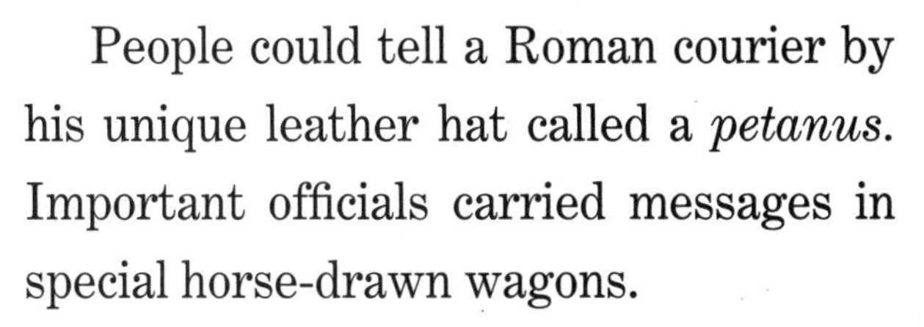

People could tell a Roman courier by his unique leather hat called a *petanus*. Important officials carried messages in special horse-drawn wagons.

At last it was possible for ordinary Romans to find out urgent news. They also hired private messengers to send letters to family and friends.

Some of the Roman letters from a thousand years ago still exist. They sound like letters and emails today. There are some from soldiers to their families telling them they were well and asking for new socks!

The Mail Goes On

People all over the world used horses to carry mail. More than 800 years ago, the Chinese had thousands of miles of roads. They also had great mail service. There were over 25,000 relay stations just to handle the mail. Think how many horses that took!

From the 1500s to the late 1800s, thousands of couriers and their horses galloped along roads throughout Spain, Germany, Austria, Italy, and Hungary.

Pony Express

Until 1860, most mail in the United States went by stagecoaches pulled by teams of

Richard Erastus Egan was an eighteen-year-old Pony Express rider. He once got caught in a terrible snowstorm and became so turned around he wound up back where he started.

strong horses. It took months for mail in the United States to get from the West Coast to the East Coast in wagons or by boat. Trains didn't travel that far, and telegraph lines didn't reach from coast to coast.

The telegraph sent messages through wires strung over great distances.

Some businessmen set up a system to deliver mail from Missouri to California in less than fourteen days. They built stations every ten to fifteen miles. They also bought four hundred horses known for speed and endurance, including mustangs or Thoroughbreds. Then they hired eighty young riders. Many were teenagers.

The riders were expert horsemen. Some were only fifteen, and there are reports of one eleven-year-old! They rode nonstop for seventy-five to one hundred miles before a new rider took over.

The entire route was about 1,900 miles long.

The men stopped at stations every fifteen miles for a fresh horse. They leapt off one horse and onto the back of another in a flash!

The Pony Express lasted only nineteen months before telegraph lines were completed to take its place. Express riders covered a total of 650,000 miles. That's like going around the earth about twenty-six times! They delivered over 35,000 pieces of mail and only lost one packet of letters. The riders and their horses endured harsh weather and sometimes had to outrun bandits or hostile Native tribes. Most people would agree that Pony Express riders and their amazing horses were true American heroes!

Riders carried twenty pounds of mail.

Turn the page to learn about an ancient Chinese route.

The Tea Horse Road

The Tea Horse Road wasn't actually a road. It was a series of paths covering almost 1,400 miles from China to Tibet. Beginning about a thousand years ago, men, women, and mules hauled millions of pounds of tea from China to trade for Tibetan horses. The trails were very dangerous. The workers faced raging rivers, steep valleys, rain, snow, and mountain passes 17,000 feet high. Some carried loads of over 300 pounds on their backs.

When they got to Tibet, tea was traded for horses. The Tibetans bred strong, fine horses. The Chinese needed them to fight off hordes of nomad raiders. At certain times as many as 25,000 horses a year arrived in China from Tibet!

The trade in horses continued until the end of the 1800s. After that, the Chinese traded tea for goods like gold, medicine, silver, and cloth. Traffic on the trails didn't stop until 1949. Today much of the trail has disappeared and is covered with weeds or concrete highways.

5

Warhorses

Men and horses began fighting together about 5,000 years ago. The type of warhorses soldiers used depended on what jobs needed to be done. Some horses pulled heavy supply wagons or war chariots. Others were strong and fast so that soldiers could fight on horseback and move around the battlefield easily.

The first warhorses pulled chariots. The ancient Greeks, Romans, Indians, Chinese, Arabs, and Egyptians all used chariots.

Soldiers drove them into combat and either shot arrows from the chariots or leapt out to fight on the ground.

Chariot Battles

In the Battle of Kadesh between the Egyptians and the Hittites about 3,000 years ago, between 5,000 and 6,000 chariots were on the battlefield!

Two thousand years ago, Julius Caesar wrote about a battle between Roman and British soldiers. He said that the British chariot horses would dash into battle at full speed to create confusion and could stop and turn in a split second.

As time passed, soldiers stopped using chariots. Improvements in bows and other weapons made fighting on horseback a better choice. The last chariot battle was in Scotland almost 2,000 years ago.

This famous mosaic from the ruins of the Roman city Pompeii shows a chariot battle.

Training Warhorses

In the heat of battle, soldiers couldn't take time to control their horses. Horses were perfectly trained to endure noise, fighting, and chaos. They had to obey a simple tug of the reins and the changing positions of the rider's legs and feet.

Xenophon was a Greek soldier who lived thousands of years ago. He wrote the first book on training warhorses. To teach them to jump over ditches, Xenophon suggested the trainer first show the ditch to the horse. Then he needed to jump over it himself. After the horse learned to jump small ditches, the trainer was to take it over bigger jumps. He also advised soldiers to play mock war games with other horses and riders and hunt whenever possible.

Bucephalus

Two thousand years ago, King Philip II ruled Macedonia. King Philip was a powerful king with a young son named Alexander.

Macedonia today is in northern Greece.

The famous writer Plutarch wrote that a horse seller tried to sell King Philip II a splendid wild stallion. He was all black except for a white patch shaped like a star on his forehead.

The horse was so fierce that no one could approach him. King Philip II refused to buy the animal. Alexander was about twelve at the time. He told his father he wanted to buy the horse and was

positive he could tame him. Philip II and his men laughed and made fun of the boy.

Alexander saw that the horse was afraid of shadows. He gently turned him to face the sun. Then Alexander began to

stroke and talk to him. In one skillful leap, the boy bounded onto the horse's back. Speaking gently to him, Alexander coaxed the stallion into a gallop. From then on, Alexander was the only person who could ever ride him. He was called Bucephalus (byoo-SEFF-uh-liss), which meant *ox head*.

Alexander is called Alexander the Great.

Alexander became a great leader who conquered much of the known world. He and Bucephalus went through many bloody battles together. When his loyal horse died, Alexander was heartbroken and named a city in his honor.

Knights and Horses

The Middle Ages began in about 1100 and lasted until about 1450. During this time, kings ruled Europe. They were often at war with each other. Knights were warriors who fought for a king and got land and other favors for their loyalty.

A knight had to have a big, strong horse. He wore heavy armor that sometimes weighed over one hundred pounds. His helmet alone could weigh forty pounds! If a knight fell off his horse, he had big trouble getting back up!

Soldiers and horses in heavy armor belonged to fighting units called the heavy cavalry.

The horse wore a padded cloth over its back and metal armor around its head, body, neck, and chest.

Because a knight fought with a sword or lance in his hands, he guided his horse with pressure from his legs. The horse was trained to charge into battle and even to bite, kick, and trample down the enemy!

The bond between a knight and his horse was powerful. A horse often stood guard for long periods over a knight lying wounded on the ground.

In the late 1300s, armies began to fight with cannons and other weapons. The days of knights came to an end.

The Chinese were the first to use cannons.

After the Knights

For hundreds of years afterward, soldiers still fought battles with horses.

General Robert E. Lee could see the battlefield from the back of his faithful horse, Traveller.

Only now they fought with pistols and sabers instead of swords and heavy armor. Without armor, soldiers could ride lighter, faster horses that could get on and off the battlefield quickly.

Horses were heroes in the American Civil War, which lasted from 1861 to 1865. They carried officers into battle, delivered messages, and helped soldiers raid and spy on the enemy. They also pulled supply wagons. By the time the war was over, a million horses and mules had died.

After World War I ended in 1918, trucks, jeeps, and tanks began to replace horses. Millions of soldiers died in that terrible war. And millions of horses did as well. Although some horses were used in later wars, the military never needed them again in any great number. The days when brave warhorses and soldiers faced the enemy together had come to an end.

Reckless

Reckless was a little mare in the Korean War in the fifties. A marine officer bought her from a racetrack to carry guns for American soldiers fighting the North Koreans.

The marines trained Reckless to ignore the noise of guns and bombs. Reckless became part of the marines' lives. She ate scrambled eggs and drank coffee with them in the morning!

In 1953, there was a dreadful battle. Marines were trapped on a mountain and needed Reckless to keep them supplied with guns and bullets. They also needed her to carry wounded or dead soldiers down the mountain. One day, Reckless walked over rice paddies and down the mountain over fifty-one times, often by herself.

She carried a total of five tons of ammunition and covered over thirty-five miles! Shells and bombs whizzed over her head, and she was slightly wounded twice. Even with five hundred shells landing every minute, the little horse never gave up.

After the war, Reckless was honored and given the rank of sergeant. A famous magazine listed Reckless as one of the greatest heroes in American history.

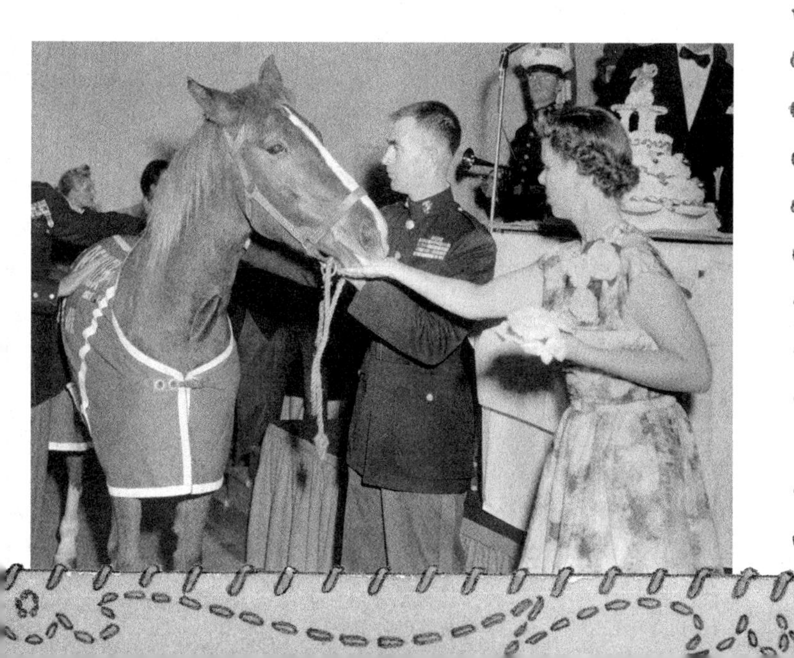

6

Famous Horses

Throughout history, certain horses have captured our hearts. Some were courageous warhorses. Others are the stuff of myths and folktales. There are also horses that made their name in sports or in movies and television.

In the forties and fifties, many kids watched cowboy movies. They especially liked Roy Rogers and his golden palomino horse, Trigger. Roy owned Trigger and made a lot of movies with him.

In almost all his movies, Trigger wore a special silver and gold saddle. Sometimes Roy sent the saddle to stores around the country so all his fans could see it. It was kept in a locked case with armed guards standing by.

Trigger was a smart horse. He could untie knots and do other tricks. He could even do the hula! He was so famous that there was a comic book about his adventures. When Trigger died in 1965, Roy had him stuffed and put on display for everyone to see.

Napoléon's Horse

Napoléon I of France ruled his country from 1804 to 1815. He was a great general who conquered many lands. Napoléon loved horses, but he didn't ride well.

Napoléon had a heroic and patient horse named Marengo. There are many stories about Napoléon and Marengo and the battles they rode into. Marengo was wounded at least eight times. During Napoléon's attack on Russia, Marengo carried him 3,000 miles. Napoléon said that when he got lost, he'd drop his reins, and Marengo would figure out where to go.

Horse Tales

In England, children used to read adventure stories about Dick Turpin and his horse, Black Bess. Dick was a real bandit who robbed travelers along the roads in England in the early 1700s. However, many of the stories about him came from people's imaginations.

It was said that on a dark night, Dick robbed a man of a beautiful black mare. He named her Black Bess. There are many stories and songs about Dick's adventures with this incredible horse. In one, Black Bess and Dick galloped two hundred miles from London to York without stopping! (Impossible!)

No one knows if Black Bess existed. One story claimed that she ran faster than an eagle could fly. (Maybe that's proof enough that she really didn't exist.)

Dan Patch

From 1905 until he died in 1916, Dan Patch was the most famous racehorse around. He was a champion harness racer that never lost a race.

In harness racing, a driver sits in a small two-wheeled cart called a sulky. The horse that pulls the cart is called a pacer. Pacers don't gallop. They are bred for a special gait called a pace, which is like a trot. Pacers can reach speeds of twenty-five to thirty miles an hour!

Dan Patch broke at least fourteen world speed records. As many as 100,000 people came to see him when he went on tours. Dan Patch rode in his own elegant railroad car. When the train pulled into town, crowds lined up along the tracks.

Dan Patch was in magazine ads for things like washing machines, coffee, and toys. One year he made over a million dol-

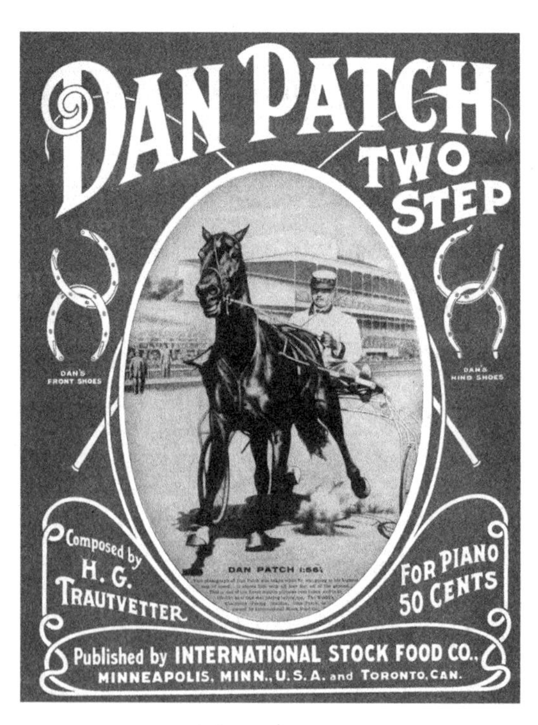

Dan Patch even had a song named after him! This is the cover of the sheet music for the "Dan Patch Two Step."

lars for his owner! After he died in 1916, a newspaper writer said that there had never been a kinder, wiser horse.

Horses have been a part of our lives for so long that there are hundreds of stories about them. Some are true. Others are just great stories.

Walk, trot, and gallop
along with us to nuzzle
some famous horses!

Pegasus, the Myth

Pegasus was a favorite horse of the Greek gods. He flew through the sky on silver and white wings. Whenever Pegasus tapped on the ground, sweet streams of water bubbled to the surface.

One day, a hero named Bellerophon captured the beautiful horse as he was drinking. He leapt on Pegasus's back, and the two soared through the clouds. Bellerophon was on a quest to kill a hideous monster called the Chimera. The beast had a lion's body, a tail ending in a snake's head, and a head like a goat.

Bellerophon fought and killed the Chimera. Afterward, he felt so important that

he ordered Pegasus to fly him to Olympus to live with the gods. Pegasus knew Bellerophon had grown too proud. With one quick movement, Pegasus dashed him to the ground. Bellerophon lost everything. He was alone for the rest of his life and never rode the beautiful winged horse again.

Incitatus, the Spoiled

The Roman emperor Caligula ruled almost 2,000 years ago. Caligula was cruel and killed many innocent people. Some said that the only thing he really loved was his stallion, Incitatus. Caligula loved him so much that he ordered eighteen servants to see to the horse's every need. He also made Roman officials come to dinner parties in the stable, insisting that Incitatus was the host.

Incitatus lived in a marble stable with an ivory manger and chomped on oats sprinkled with gold dust. Caligula paraded him around in a purple blanket and a collar of fine jewels. One story said that Caligula demanded that Incitatus be elected a consul, the most important job in the Roman government.

When the stallion died, Caligula held a big funeral for him. And if that wasn't enough, he ordered everyone to worship Incitatus as a god!

Cholla was an angry horse named for a prickly cactus. He had been trained by cowboys in a very harsh way. In 1990, just before he turned five, a woman named Renee Chambers bought him. Renee treated him kindly, and Cholla began to trust her and calm down.

Once, when Renee was painting a fence on her ranch, she noticed that Cholla followed her around to watch. He seemed so interested that Renee tacked a piece of paper to a fence post and mixed up some watercolors. Then she put a brush in Cholla's mouth. He didn't chew it up or spit it out. Instead, he held it carefully and began painting! Cholla is still painting today.

When Cholla paints, he picks out the brush he wants and chooses his colors. Using his tongue and teeth to control the brush, he can paint in different directions. A few years ago, thirty of his watercolors were in a special art show in Venice, Italy!

Beautiful Jim Key, the Smartest

There's never been a horse as smart as Beautiful Jim Key. He was born in the late 1800s. His owner, Dr. William Key, was a wonderful horse trainer and a former slave. William knew that Beautiful Jim had a great brain. Using gentle methods, William taught him to recognize numbers and letters. Then they went around the country putting on shows.

Using alphabet and number blocks, Beautiful Jim could count, point to letters in a name with his nose, sort mail, and give correct change from a cash register. He could also do math problems. One of his best tricks was to take a coin out of a water bucket without drinking the water or spilling a drop!

At the St. Louis World's Fair in 1904, Beautiful Jim awed the crowds. Among them was Alice Roosevelt, President Teddy Roosevelt's daughter. Beautiful Jim spelled her name by picking out letters in the alphabet. To this day, no one can explain Beautiful Jim's genius.

Seabiscuit, the Winner

Seabiscuit was a Thoroughbred born in 1933. When he was young, his owners raced him too often. Although he was in a lot of races, he didn't win many of them. A great horse trainer named Tom Smith noticed that Seabiscuit might become a fine racehorse. But the horse was tired, sore, and in need of rest and a good diet.

Tom trained Seabiscuit, and with the help of a jockey named Johnny "Red" Pollard, brought him back to health. Red was taller than most jockeys. He was also blind in one eye. He couldn't even see which horses were running ahead of him.

Seabiscuit and Red began to win lots of

races. Unlike most horses, Seabiscuit sped up at the end of races. He loved to win! Before long, fans all over the country were following Seabiscuit's career.

In 1938, in Seabiscuit's greatest race, he beat a champion named War Admiral. Seabiscuit's last race was in 1940. Around seventy-five thousand people jammed the track in California to cheer him on. That day, Seabiscuit broke the track's speed record. The great horse died in 1947.

7

Horses in Sports

There have been sporting events for horses ever since they were first tamed. Tribes in Central Asia raced horses about 6,000 years ago. Horse racing is still popular all over the world. In the United States, almost half the states have racetracks. Millions flock to them every year.

The most famous race in America is the Kentucky Derby, which has been held since 1875. About twenty Thoroughbreds and their jockeys thunder down the track at speeds of up to about forty-five miles an hour. The racecourse covers a mile and a quarter and takes only two minutes. It is often called the most exciting two minutes in all of sports.

Thoroughbreds and quarter horses are the fastest racers.

Thoroughbred racing began in England about three hundred years ago. It's still going strong today. Queen Elizabeth II loves horses and owns several racehorses. Once, when her horse won, people spotted the queen jumping up and down and clapping her hands!

Only Thoroughbreds compete in the Kentucky Derby, but other breeds, like the American quarter horse, run in many other races.

The Olympics

Almost 3,000 years ago, chariot racing in the ancient Greek Olympics was a very popular sport. *Equestrian,* or horse-related, events have been in the modern Olympic Games since 1912. Today men and women compete as equals in these contests.

Horses are the only animals in the Olympics. The medal goes to the horse and rider.

The three equestrian sports in the Olympics are *show jumping, dressage,* and *eventing* contests. In show jumping, horses race around a course with about fifteen fences, or jumps. The riders get a penalty every time their horse hits one of the jumps or refuses to go over it. Horses and riders with the fastest times and the fewest penalties win.

Queen Elizabeth II's daughter and granddaughter have both been Olympic medal winners.

The sport of dressage (druh-SAHJ) began many years ago with the training of military horses. In dressage, a rider guides his horse through a series of movements. The horse must obey the slightest pressure from the rider's legs, hands, and body. During the event, a horse's and rider's movements must be relaxed and smooth.

Anky van Grunsven and her horse, Salinero, won the gold medal for dressage at the 2008 Olympics.

Eventing tests horses and riders to their limits. The competition usually lasts three days. The contests include cross-country racing along with jumping and dressage. Eventing requires horses and riders with speed, endurance, and bravery.

Show Jumping

Show jumping is not just for the Olympics. There are show jumping events all over the country. Many are for kids.

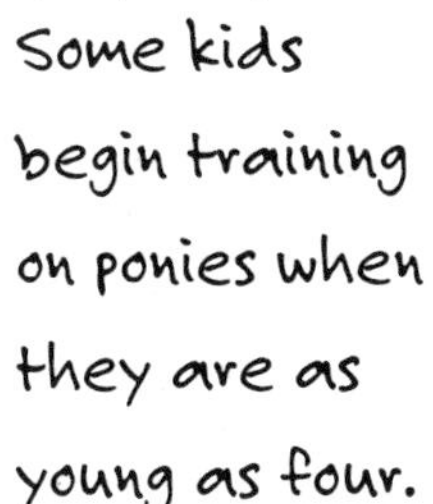

Some kids begin training on ponies when they are as young as four.

Riders first learn to jump by trotting over poles lying on the ground. This teaches them to sit properly and keep their balance. The first jump they take is only about eighteen inches high. When riders are expert enough, they begin going over a series of jumps. Riders must control their horses and, after they finish one jump, prepare them to take the next.

Rodeos

Rodeos began many years ago when cowboys had contests based on their everyday chores. Today rodeos are still popular for men and women and even kids. And you don't have to be a cowboy to compete—you just have to

ride like one! Some rodeos are only for fun; others offer cash prizes to the winners.

Contests like calf roping, bucking-bronco riding, and steer wrestling are still based on ranch work. Other popular events like barrel racing and bull riding test riders' skill and bravery.

There are many other sports for riders and horses. Some people compete in harness or carriage events. Others ride in cross-country races or play a game called polo. But many people of all ages ride just because they really enjoy it.

The Amazing Lis Hartel

Lis Hartel was born in Denmark in 1921. As a girl, she competed in both dressage and show jumping. When Lis was twenty-two, she got a terrible disease called polio. Lis survived but was paralyzed from her knees down for the rest of her life.

Doctors told her she would never ride again. They were wrong! A few years later, in 1952, Lis was one of the first women to compete in equestrian events in the Olympics. She won a silver medal in dressage. Four years later, in the 1956 Olympics, she won another silver medal for the same event! Lis spent the rest of her life encouraging and teaching disabled people to ride. She died at the age of eighty-seven in 2009.

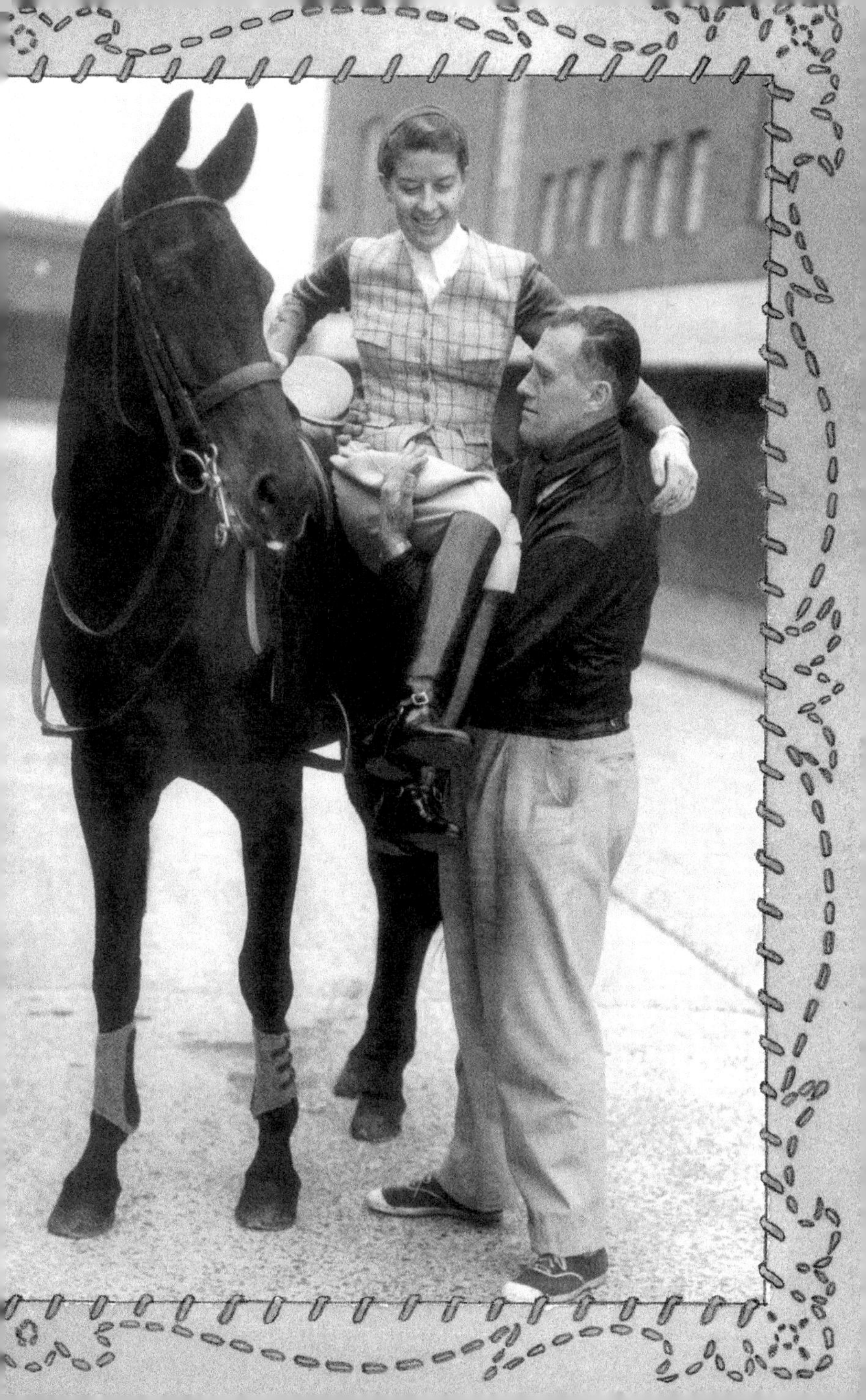

8

Different Needs for Horses

A little over one hundred years ago, horses were still a big part of our world. Almost everything we bought and everywhere we went depended on their labor. Cities were packed with people and horses.

New York City, for example, had passenger coaches and railroad cars pulled by horses. Sometimes they carried as many as 120,000 people a day! These vehicles, plus horses and mules pulling other carriages and wagons, created terrible traffic jams. Pollution from horse dung was a major health problem. When it rained, rivers of manure flowed down the pavement.

Twentieth-Century Changes

The invention of cars and trucks in the early 1900s almost put an end to horse-drawn vehicles. A new age had begun when we no longer depended on horses in our daily lives.

Today horses might not work as hard for us as they once did, but they are still part of our lives. There are about seven million horses in the United States today. People keep them to ride for pleasure, or for horse shows, for sports, and for other jobs as well.

Police officers use horses for crowd

control and to patrol parts of cities. Some park rangers ride horses into wilderness areas that have no roads. There are still places where horses plow fields and clear timber in forests. In many countries, like Afghanistan, horses continue to work as pack animals.

Therapy Horses

Horses have a new job. All over the United States, there are stables with trained horses that take disabled people riding. Experts explain that many of these people, especially kids, are more comfortable on horseback. The rocking motion and the horse's large, warm body soothe them.

Some autistic children seem to feel happier up on a horse than they do on the ground. Horseback riding can also

change their behavior. Many children seem calmer and smile a lot more when they're on a horse.

Horses are animals with intelligence, loyalty, and bravery. They have good memories and strong feelings for people and other horses. Research shows that they know certain words and remember instructions for ten years or longer. Horses can recognize people and other horses even after they've been apart for a long time. Horses sometimes bond with each other for life. Throughout our long history together, horses have given us so much. For the people who love them, every horse is a hero.

Doing More Research

There's a lot more you can learn about horses. The fun of research is seeing how many different sources you can explore.

Books 

Most libraries and bookstores have books about horses.

Here are some things to remember when you're using books for research:

1. You don't have to read the whole book. Check the table of contents and the index to find the topics you're interested in.

2. Write down the name of the book.

When you take notes, make sure you write down the name of the book in your notebook so you can find it again.

3. Never copy exactly from a book.

When you learn something new from a book, put it in your own words.

4. Make sure the book is nonfiction.

Some books tell make-believe stories about horses. Make-believe stories are called *fiction.* They're fun to read, but not good for research.

Research books have facts and tell true stories. They are called *nonfiction.* A librarian or teacher can help you make sure the books you use for research are nonfiction.

Here are some good non-fiction books about horses:

- *Everything Horse*, Kids' FAQs series, by Marty Crisp
- *Gunner: Hurricane Horse*, True Horse Stories series, by Judy Andrekson
- *Horse*, a DK Eyewitness Book, by Juliet Clutton-Brock
- *Horse & Pony Factfile* by Sandy Ransford and the editors of Kingfisher
- *Horse Crazy! 1,001 Fun Facts, Craft Projects, Games, Activities, and Know-How for Horse-Loving Kids* by Jessie Haas
- *I Wonder Why Horses Wear Shoes and Other Questions About Horses*, I Wonder Why series, by Jackie Gaff

Museums and Parks

Many museums and parks have exhibits about horses. These places can help you learn more about horses.

When you go to a museum or park:

1. Be sure to take your notebook!

Write down anything that catches your interest. Draw pictures, too!

2. Ask questions.

There are almost always people at museums and parks who can help you find what you're looking for.

3. Check the calendar.

Many museums and parks have special events and activities just for kids!

Here are some museums and parks that have exhibits about horses:

- American Quarter Horse Hall of Fame and Museum (Amarillo, Texas)
- Hubbard Museum of the American West (Ruidoso Downs, New Mexico)
- International Museum of the Horse (Lexington, Kentucky)
- Kentucky Horse Park (Lexington)
- National Museum of Racing and Hall of Fame (Saratoga Springs, New York)
- National Museum of the American Indian (Washington, D.C.)
- Pony Express National Museum (St. Joseph, Missouri)

DVDs

There are some great nonfiction DVDs about horses. As with books, make sure the DVDs you watch for research are nonfiction!

Check your library or video store for these and other non-fiction titles about horses:

- *Cloud: Wild Stallion of the Rockies* from NATURE
- *Horse Power: Road to Maclay* from Animal Planet
- KidsLoveAnimals.com's *African Safari* from Stone Canyon Productions
- *The Noble Horse* from National Geographic
- *World of Horses* from Discovery Channel

The Internet

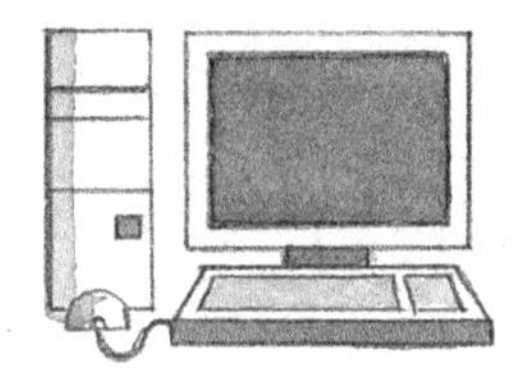

Many websites have lots of facts about horses. Some also have games and activities that can help make learning about horses even more fun.

Ask your teacher or your parents to help you find more websites like these:

- amnh.org/exhibitions/past-exhibitions/horse
- animals.howstuffworks.com/mammals/horse-info
- blazekids.com
- enchantedlearning.com/themes/horse
- historyforkids.org/learn/environment/horses.htm
- medievaleurope.mrdonn.org/jousts.html

Good luck!

Index

Photographs courtesy of:

Have you read the adventure that matches up with this book?

Don't miss

Magic Tree House® Merlin Mission #21

STALLION BY STARLIGHT

When the magic tree house whisks them to ancient Macedonia, Jack and Annie meet a young Alexander the Great and a beautiful black stallion that no one can tame. What is the connection between Alexander and the stallion? And how can Jack and Annie help them both?

Magic Tree House®

#1: Dinosaurs Before Dark
#2: The Knight at Dawn
#3: Mummies in the Morning
#4: Pirates Past Noon
#5: Night of the Ninjas
#6: Afternoon on the Amazon
#7: Sunset of the Sabertooth
#8: Midnight on the Moon
#9: Dolphins at Daybreak
#10: Ghost Town at Sundown
#11: Lions at Lunchtime
#12: Polar Bears Past Bedtime
#13: Vacation Under the Volcano
#14: Day of the Dragon King
#15: Viking Ships at Sunrise
#16: Hour of the Olympics
#17: Tonight on the *Titanic*
#18: Buffalo Before Breakfast
#19: Tigers at Twilight
#20: Dingoes at Dinnertime
#21: Civil War on Sunday
#22: Revolutionary War on Wednesday
#23: Twister on Tuesday
#24: Earthquake in the Early Morning
#25: Stage Fright on a Summer Night
#26: Good Morning, Gorillas
#27: Thanksgiving on Thursday
#28: High Tide in Hawaii

Magic Tree House® Merlin Missions

#1: Christmas in Camelot
#2: Haunted Castle on Hallows Eve
#3: Summer of the Sea Serpent
#4: Winter of the Ice Wizard
#5: Carnival at Candlelight
#6: Season of the Sandstorms
#7: Night of the New Magicians
#8: Blizzard of the Blue Moon
#9: Dragon of the Red Dawn
#10: Monday with a Mad Genius
#11: Dark Day in the Deep Sea
#12: Eve of the Emperor Penguin
#13: Moonlight on the Magic Flute
#14: A Good Night for Ghosts
#15: Leprechaun in Late Winter
#16: A Ghost Tale for Christmas Time
#17: A Crazy Day with Cobras
#18: Dogs in the Dead of Night
#19: Abe Lincoln at Last!
#20: A Perfect Time for Pandas
#21: Stallion by Starlight
#22: Hurry Up, Houdini!
#23: High Time for Heroes
#24: Soccer on Sunday
#25: Shadow of the Shark
#26: Balto of the Blue Dawn
#27: Night of the Ninth Dragon

Magic Tree House®
Super Edition

#1: World at War, 1944

Magic Tree House®
Fact Trackers

Dinosaurs
Knights and Castles
Mummies and Pyramids
Pirates
Rain Forests
Space
Titanic
Twisters and Other Terrible Storms
Dolphins and Sharks
Ancient Greece and the Olympics
American Revolution
Sabertooths and the Ice Age
Pilgrims
Ancient Rome and Pompeii
Tsunamis and Other Natural Disasters
Polar Bears and the Arctic
Sea Monsters
Penguins and Antarctica
Leonardo da Vinci
Ghosts
Leprechauns and Irish Folklore
Rags and Riches: Kids in the Time of Charles Dickens
Snakes and Other Reptiles
Dog Heroes
Abraham Lincoln
Pandas and Other Endangered Species
Horse Heroes
Heroes for All Times
Soccer
Ninjas and Samurai
China: Land of the Emperor's Great Wall
Sharks and Other Predators
Vikings
Dogsledding and Extreme Sports
Dragons and Mythical Creatures
World War II

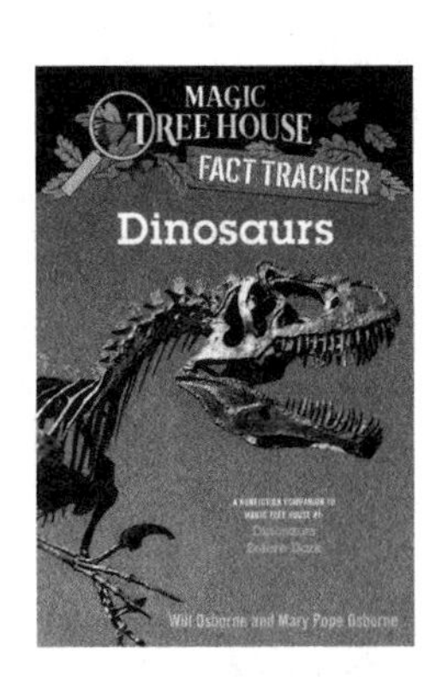

More Magic Tree House®

Games and Puzzles from the Tree House
Magic Tricks from the Tree House
My Magic Tree House Journal
Magic Tree House Survival Guide
Animal Games and Puzzles
Magic Tree House Incredible Fact Book

CALLING ALL ADVENTURERS!
Join the
MAGIC TREE HOUSE®
KIDS' ADVENTURE CLUB
Members receive:
• Exclusive packages delivered throughout the year
• Members-only swag
• A sneak peek at upcoming books
• Access to printables, games, giveaways, and more!
With a parent's help, visit MagicTreeHouse.com to learn more and to sign up!
© 2016 Mary Pope Osborne. Magic Tree House is a registered trademark of Mary Pope Osborne; used under license. Illustrations © 2016 by Sal Murdocca.
RHCB
MagicTreeHouse.com